General William Palmer
Railroad Pioneer

General William Palmer
Railroad Pioneer

A NOW YOU KNOW BIO

Number Thirteen in the Series

Joyce B. Lohse

Filter Press, LLC
Palmer Lake, Colorado

Dedicated
to Charlie's children
and to all who love trains.

ISBN: 978-0-86541-092-3
Library of Congress Control Number: 2009923991
Copyright © 2009 Joyce B. Lohse. All Rights Reserved.

Cover photograph of William J. Palmer by Harry Standley, undated, courtesy
Colorado College Special Collections.

Back cover photograph of Glen Eyrie courtesy Joyce B. Lohse.

General William Palmer: Railroad Pioneer
Published by
Filter Press, LLC, P.O. Box 95, Palmer Lake, CO 80133
719-481-2420   info@FilterPressBooks.com

Printed in the United States of America

Contents

William Jackson Palmer, 1836 – 1909

1 Railroad Dreams

In the mid-1800s, a new sound floated through the air inviting thoughts of faraway places and visions of adventures waiting to happen. That new sound was distant train whistles. Train engines powered by steam were new on the American landscape. The first successful commercial **locomotive** was introduced in America in 1829. America was busy building rails for the new method of travel.

During the same period, **Manifest Destiny** was on the minds of Americans. The idea that the United States was destined to extend from the Atlantic to Pacific Oceans gave many the incentive to travel into new and unsettled territory. Able bodied young men were encouraged to "Go West" to settle the new land and find jobs as builders and pathfinders. Young people found adventure and fulfilled their own goals and dreams while helping the country expand and prosper. It is easy to imagine a curious young boy listening to a train whistle in the distance. He might wonder where the train was going and what the passengers would see and experience during their journeys.

William Jackson Palmer lived on Kinsale Farm, two miles from the town of Leipsic in Kent County, Delaware. Born on September 17, 1836, he was the second of four children. He had two brothers, Francis and Charles, and an older sister, Ellen.

Farm children had busy lives. As soon as they were able, they carried food and water to the animals, gathered eggs, or helped in the fields and the garden. All eyes were on the weather as the family watched for rain, which helped crops grow and provided water for the livestock. Dark clouds could also bring foul weather or even hurricanes.

As a young child, Palmer developed a lifelong love of animals. He always kept livestock and pets close by. Living on a farm, he learned about plants and the wonders of nature and the out-of-doors. Later in life, Palmer built city parks. He created outdoor space for "children to play—and all be refreshed by a little taste of country, without going too far afield."

In 1841, William's parents, John and Matilda Palmer, moved with their four youngsters from their Delaware farm to the nearby city of Philadelphia, Pennsylvania. Although the Palmers missed farm life and the animals, the bustling city offered more opportunities. William's father, and later his brother, Francis, went to work as tea traders.

Religion was very important to the Palmer family. They were **Quakers,** a religion also known as the Religious Society of Friends. They belonged to a **liberal branch** known as Hicksites. Monthly meetings rotated from one household to another for discussion and worship.

When they moved to Philadelphia, the Palmers asked the Quakers in their meeting group for "clearness." This meant their bills were paid and financial obligations met, and they were free to join a new monthly meeting group. Young William Palmer was a Quaker because he was the child of Quaker parents, as they before him. At Quaker meetings, he learned to value racial equality, peace, and education.

When the children were old enough, the Palmers

enrolled them in the Zane Street Friends School in Philadelphia. The Friends School reinforced their **straight-laced** and strict Quaker upbringing. Bright and curious, William studied his lessons carefully.

Know More!

Quakers in Pennsylvania

Quaker is another name for the Religious Society of Friends. Known for their **humanitarian** activities, Quakers reject war in favor of peace, support racial equality, and encourage quality education. George Fox was founder of Quakerism in England. The word *Quaker* resulted when Fox told a judge to "tremble at the Word of the Lord," and the judge responded by calling him a "quaker."

William Penn received a charter from the King of England in 1681 to establish a Quaker colony in Pennsylvania. The peace-loving Quakers governed the colony until 1756 and maintained only a small police force. It was a safe place that provided a sanctuary for Quakers to practice their religion. In 1828, liberal Hicksite Quakers separated from conservative Orthodox Quakers.

Quakers practice no special acts or rituals, believing that their religion is a part of everyday life. Instead, they gather for business meetings and worship at monthly, quarterly, and yearly gatherings guided by a Clerk. Originally, Quaker meetings included long periods of silent meditation.

Perhaps William Palmer knew he was destined for engineering greatness. He attended Central High School in Philadelphia, a prestigious institution which still exists. Only the brightest and hardest working students who passed rigorous admission exams continued their studies at the school. One day he would use his education to build a railroad empire in the Great American West.

2 Travels Abroad

William Palmer's education did not end when he finished school. He completed engineering classes and became a **surveyor** at age seventeen. His first job was with the Hempfield Railroad. Palmer walked for miles through the rolling hills of western Pennsylvania to study the land and plan the best routes for railroads.

William was still a teenager when his uncle, F. H. Jackson of the Westmoreland Coal Company, suggested he travel to Europe to study transportation, fuel systems, and the use of coal. To help pay for the trip, William wrote articles for the *Miner's Journal* magazine for four dollars per article.

William left home excited and a little scared. He wrote:

…I shouldered my **traps** one rainy June morning and marched down to the *Tuscarora,* [the ship] half afraid she was gone, half afraid of going in her…The three weeks of ship life spent between Delaware Bay and the Mersey [river near Liverpool, England] are only remembered as a little period of fun and danger and novelty to be recalled in the future as an experience of things which are happening every day yet unknown to those who stay at home.

The trip was the beginning of William's lifelong love of travel and adventure.

Palmer's travels abroad served two purposes. First, he gained practical experience as a railroad **apprentice.** Second, he met important people and gathered information that later would help him build his own railroads.

At eighteen years old, William was somewhat shy and loved to write. His bound journals were filled with engineering notes. Carefully penned letters home filled every space on the paper from edge to edge. His descriptions of Paris written to his sister were so lengthy that he decided to carry the packet of pages home rather than pay for postage.

Palmer's 1855 journals burst with details about everyday life in England. Perhaps he was already visualizing towns and services along new train routes. When he rode the train, Palmer noted how many wheels, how many drivers, the gauge of road, weight of rails, how far apart the sleepers, how shallow the furnace. He was especially interested in smokeless fuel, comparing **anthracite** from England to coal from South Wales.

Palmer was expected to have **letters of introduction** when he visited railroad companies and other industrial sites. It was difficult to visit businessmen without the letters. He wrote in his journal about a failed attempt to visit a soap maker in England:

> Peyton & Roberts Soap, Wapping [England], Jan/55
>
> Called & stated that I was an American & requested permission to inspect smoke consumer. Parkers [the type of equipment]
>
> 'Have you got an introduction?' No.
>
> 'We shall expect to have an introduction before we can open our door to strangers. Else you let everyone come.'
>
> 'Ah – good morning.'

Palmer moved on, quickly putting the rejection behind.

Palmer entertained his family with lengthy essays describing British customs. A letter of introduction led him to stay in the household of a family acquaintance named Mr. Morgan in Wales. In a letter to his family, he described breakfast in the home.

The family consisting of his wife and her servant, Mr. Morgan and a temporary resident in the shape of a nephew about to enter in the army, with myself, rose about 8 in the morning. Cold meat, toast, eggs, tea and bread and butter were brought in by the servant about half past eight or nine, and Everyone sat down as he dropped in, without the slightest ceremony or *fuss* whatever, as each one entered the pleasant *salle a manger* [dining room] warmed by a cheerful grate burning *stone* coal, the rest arose and shook hands with him bidding him Good Morning. This was a decidedly pleasant and cheerful social custom and ought to be introduced on the other side [of] the water, where we half the time carelessly interchange a 'good morning' and as often as not forget or omit it altogether.

While visiting Wales, Palmer wrote about the advantages of coal as fuel in a letter to a Welsh newspaper. When it was published, he became anxious and worried that the letter would be criticized. "I began to tremble at having done such an awfully tremendous thing and wished it were undone. But there was no help for it thereafter." As time went by, he learned to have confidence in his opinions.

At the end of one lengthy letter home, Palmer explained plans to extend his travels to Paris before returning to England and on to the United States. A contact provided him with a "great batch of letters of introduction," which opened doors for further visits and study. He was meeting new business contacts and learning to raise money from investors. This skill would be useful later when he needed investors for railroad construction.

Palmer returned home to Pennsylvania and resumed working for the Westmoreland Coal Company. Later he took a job with the Pennsylvania Central Railroad for $900 a year. He was secretary to company president, J. Edgar Thomson, who had supervised his **apprenticeship** in Europe.

Palmer was also interested in politics. With his friend Isaac Clothier, he organized a series of lectures called "The Young Men's Liberal Course of Lectures." During one presentation, "The Present Aspect of the Slavery Question," **dissenters** threatened to cause trouble. Palmer believed in freedom of speech and continued with the presentation. The controversy taught Palmer to face and deal with confrontation, another important lesson.

The 1860 Philadelphia census listed William J. Palmer's occupation as "clerk," his position with the

Know More!

The First Locomotives

A locomotive is a machine that moves trains along railroad tracks by pushing or pulling them. Early locomotives could move only a few cars at a time. A modern locomotive can move more than 200 loaded freight cars. A road locomotive hauls freight cars, a yard switcher locomotive moves cars from track to track, and a general purpose locomotive is used for hauling or switching. Sources of locomotive power are diesel, which uses compressed air in cylinders; electric, receiving power from wires or rails; and steam, fueled by coal or oil burned in a firebox. Another type called gas turbines created the turbo train, which was powered by units built into one or more cars instead of a locomotive and is no longer used to haul freight in the United States.

railroad company. The job allowed him to help support his family. Life was never again quite as simple as it had been for the young man who went abroad in 1855.

3 Prisoner of War

After Palmer returned from Europe, he continued to work for the railroad. A few years later, Civil War threatened the United States. The country was divided between North and South over whether slavery should be allowed. Agriculture in the South depended on slave labor. In the North, many people were forced to make a choice, whether to avoid involvement in war, or to fight against slavery. This decision was not lightly made. The Quaker religion taught **pacifism.** A Quaker could be removed from the religion for joining the military.

After much thought, Palmer decided to fight. He joined the Union Army and organized a cavalry troop of handpicked men. His plan was simple. Palmer, a good rider, would lead the troops on horseback.

The "Anderson Troop" of the Fifteenth Pennsylvania Volunteer Cavalry was created in 1862 and named for General Robert Anderson. Palmer was captain of the troop. He gathered men he knew and trusted from school days in Philadelphia to serve under his command.

The four hundred soldiers of Anderson Troop were loyal to Palmer and had faith in his leadership. Out of respect for Palmer's strict Quaker beliefs, they pledged to stay away from liquor. They were an impressive group of men, confident that they would be well directed under Palmer's supervision. With pride, he wrote to his friend Isaac Clothier in Philadelphia, "I have the honor to inform you that at present I am Captain of the Troop."

The Anderson Troop's first test was at the Battle of Antietam in Maryland. Captain Palmer rode behind enemy lines to gather information about enemy troop movements. Information he collected was sent by messengers to Union Army leaders to help plan **strategy.** This was dangerous work. If caught by the Confederate Army, he could be hanged as a spy.

Following a mission in September 1862, Palmer did not return to camp. When he crossed the Potomac River to gather intelligence, a regiment of Confederate troops blocked his escape route. A young slave girl hid

The interior of a Union Army Civil War tent similar to the tents used by Anderson Troop. Reprinted from Harper's New Monthly Magazine, March 1867.

Palmer in an attic, but a careless messenger revealed his location, and he was captured.

Palmer was held prisoner in "Castle Thunder" near Richmond, Virginia. The building had been a tobacco warehouse before the war. Now it was a Confederate prison. Although some captured soldiers were delighted to find tobacco in their prison, they soon discovered that food was scarce. Living conditions were harsh, and not all the prisoners survived.

Captain Palmer cleverly hid his identity by using the name of another prisoner named "Peters." If he could avoid recognition as an officer and a spy, he would not be hanged immediately, but his future was uncertain. If only he could escape!

During his imprisonment, an article about Captain Palmer's disappearance was published in an eastern newspaper. Realizing this public announcement of his absence placed him in peril, Palmer's men made up false stories about seeing him in Washington, D.C. When the cover-up story was printed, Confederate officers naturally assumed Captain Palmer was not one of their prisoners. The plan provided a good cover and kept him temporarily safe.

Palmer and a fellow prisoner created a daring plan to escape. Each day, the two men sawed through boards under a bed using a knife blade. A hole into a vacant basement under the floorboards led to a clear route to freedom. One man sawed the boards with the crude blade while his partner covered up the noise by talking loudly and stomping his feet.

The men worked hard to cover the "zip, zip, zip"

noise the saw made. Finally, they broke through the floorboards. When they looked through, they made a terrible discovery. Duty guards surrounded their escape route. Their risky efforts were for nothing.

While Palmer was in prison, he continued to use the name "Peters." Eventually, after much confusion about his true identity, he was released from prison in exchange for Southern prisoners released from Northern prisons. He was free. His imprisonment lasted four months, from September 19, 1862, until January 15, 1863. After his release, he used his influence to arrange the release of other Union soldiers at Castle Thunder in exchange for Southern prisoners.

Palmer was promoted to the rank of colonel and rejoined his regiment in Tennessee. He soon discovered his troop was in terrible disarray. Without their leader, his handpicked elite group of soldiers had fallen apart. While Palmer was in prison, some in his unit refused to enter a battle. They felt they were not prepared to fight. Those men were jailed as traitors. Others in the troop had fought in spite of lack of direction and preparation, and had been badly beaten, wounded, or killed.

Palmer was held for four months in Castle Thunder, the infamous Confederate Civil War prison in Richmond, Virginia. Photograph showing Confederate guards is reprinted from the Photographic History of the Civil War, *volume 7, 1911.*

Palmer struggled to pull his men together again. He gathered horses, uniforms, weapons, and supplies for them. Under his guidance, his solid troop of fighting men was rebuilt. By the summer of 1864, his reorganized unit once again numbered more than three hundred men.

When William Palmer was promoted to the rank of brigadier general at twenty-nine years of age, he became one of the youngest generals in the Civil War. After the war, he was awarded the prestigious Medal of Honor for distinguished gallantry in action at Red Hill, Alabama, in 1865.

While General Palmer was a prisoner of war, Abraham Lincoln signed the Emancipation Proclamation, an executive order freeing slaves. When Southern troops continued the conflict, the Anderson Troop pursued the President of the Confederacy, Jefferson Davis. They never caught him.

After four long years, the war was over. The men could go home. General Palmer displayed courage, daring, and leadership as a cavalry officer. The army wanted him to continue as a soldier. He could have had a successful military career. Palmer had other ideas. He had done his duty to help bring an end to slavery. His dreams and plans for the future, of traveling West and building railroads, had been delayed long enough. It was time to move ahead with his plans to build towns and railroads.

Courtesy, Joyce B. Lohse

General Palmer's Civil War uniform is among many items and photographs related to Palmer's life on display in the Colorado Springs Pioneers Museum.

Know More!

The Medal of Honor

The Medal of Honor, created in 1861, is awarded by the United States Congress to members of the Armed Services who exhibit courage and gallantry while risking their life to engage in action with an enemy, in military operations, or while serving with friendly foreign forces. The person who receives the award must perform a deed of personal bravery or self-sacrifice, risking his life and performing above and beyond the call of duty. More than 3,400 people have received the Medal of Honor. One woman received the honor during the Civil War.

– Medal of Honor Citation for William J. Palmer –
With less than 200 men, attacked and defeated a superior force of the enemy, capturing their fieldpiece and about 100 prisoners without losing a man. This action took place near Red Hill, Alabama.

The Medal of Honor is an inverted five-point star decorated with clusters of laurel and oak to represent victory and strength. Thirty-four stars create a circle on the original medal, representing each of the states in 1862. They also represent the heavens and divine goals of man. Inside the circle is an image of Minerva, the goddess of wisdom and war. A male figure holding snakes represents discord and conflict. An owl on Minerva's helmet symbolizes wisdom. The ribbon holding the medal contains red for valor, hardiness, and blood; blue for vigilance, perseverance, and justice; and white for purity and innocence.

If you were asked to redesign the Medal, what would you change? What symbols would you incorporate?

4 Palmer Finds His Queen

When the Civil War ended, Palmer returned to Philadelphia. His father had died, and his family was counting on him for financial support. He needed a job. In 1867, Palmer went to St. Louis, Missouri, where he began working as a treasurer for the Kansas Pacific Railroad.

Palmer's destiny was farther west in the Rocky Mountains. When offered the chance to work as a construction manager in the West, he took it. Instead of working in a city office, he would apply his skills to the difficult management job of laying steel rails westward across the Great Plains.

The June 1867 issue of *Harper's New Monthly Magazine,* described a railroad worksite this way:

Boarding-houses for construction parties are very appropriately placed on wheels. Some are constructed like a dwelling-house, with windows, doors, etc., on three platform cars, one being fitted up for a dining-room, another for a kitchen at one end and a reception-room at the other, and the third for sleeping births. When all are run up a temporary track for use, the middle or kitchen-car is placed transversely across the track, the truck-wheels being detached, and the two other cars are brought against its opposite sides; all combined forming a comfortable dwelling-place.

Palmer's job with the Kansas Pacific Railroad required he travel long distances by train and horseback. He worked hard planning for the rapid growth of the railroad. His job was to find the financing to fund the construction and to obtain **land grants.** When one section of railroad was completed, the process to raise money and acquire land began all over again. The *Denver Post* newspaper reported in May 1867 that Palmer acquired $480,000 in United States government **bonds** to complete a thirty-mile section of railroad.

When the Kansas Pacific needed to survey land from Salina, Kansas, to San Francisco, California, in 1867-1868, Palmer accepted the challenge to lead the survey party. He relished the prospect of outdoor adventure. His job was to find the best passage through the rugged Rocky Mountains to the Pacific Coast. It would take several months by wagon train and horseback to map the new railroad routes.

During the long journey, Palmer developed an important friendship. Dr. William Bell joined the survey as official photographer. Bell was a medical student from England. He knew nothing about photography, but quickly learned to use the cumbersome **view camera** so he could travel with the survey crew. Bell and Palmer spent hours talking by the campfire, discussing future plans and sharing visions.

In July 1869, Palmer saw Pikes Peak for the first time. He was captivated by the sight. In 1921, the Colorado Springs *Gazette Telegraph* reprinted Palmer's description of his first views of the Peak, "Just before sunset we came in sight of the mountains—Pikes Peak, Spanish peaks and the Greenhorn range. A thunder storm came on and the clouds threw themselves into grand and fantastic shapes, blending with the mountain peaks so as to be indistinguishable."

Soon after he first saw Pikes Peak, Palmer wrote this prediction in his journal: "I am sure there will be a famous summer resort here soon after the railroad reaches Denver…I somehow fancy that an exploration of the dancing little tributaries of the 'Monument' or the 'Fountain' might disclose somewhere up near where they come leaping with delight from the cavernous wall of the Rocky mountains some charming spot where one perhaps might make his future home."

After the survey was completed, Palmer's next job with the Kansas Pacific was to supervise construction of the railroad line to Denver, Colorado. Under Palmer's management, an important connection from Kansas to Denver with a connection north to Cheyenne, Wyoming, was completed.

Palmer's idea was to then build a southbound railroad into Mexico. The Kansas Pacific turned down the idea. The railroad company planned to follow established east-west migration routes to the west coast. They had no interest in building a railroad into Mexico. As Palmer later wrote, "This was the first distinct conception on my part of the Denver & Rio Grande railway, which ripened into a definite plan on the completion of the Kansas Pacific railway into Denver the following year."

Palmer was captivated by Colorado Territory and the Rocky Mountains. His favorite seat when riding the stagecoach was on top with the driver. He enjoyed the open sky, regardless of the weather. He liked to watch herds of deer and antelope on the unspoiled range with a sky full of billowing clouds overhead. The Colorado Territory that Palmer saw in the 1860s was largely unsettled. Back East, people read newspaper stories and heard rumors about hardships and confrontations with Native Americans. The stories kept many people from making the difficult journey by wagon train to live in areas where the railroad had yet to expand.

During a train trip east, Palmer met a man who shared his views on extending the railroad south toward Mexico. The man was William Proctor Mellen, a lawyer from Flushing, Long Island, New York. Over the miles, Palmer found an interested listener who shared his passion for the railroad. Mellen liked the bright young man's ideas.

William Mellen was traveling with his daughter, Mary Lincoln Mellen. She was known by the nickname "Queen." Queen Mellen was born in Prestonburg, Kentucky, in 1850. When she was just four years old, her mother died. Her father remarried her mother's sister. Six more children were born. The family moved to Flushing, New York.

Queen was nineteen when she met her future husband. Palmer was thirty-two.

Queen was intelligent, witty, well-educated, loved books, music, and plays, and had a beautiful singing voice. The miles flew by as Queen and Palmer shared conversation. When William asked permission to see Queen again at her home in New York, she agreed. They were soon **courting**.

When William Palmer visited Queen in New York, he wasted no time declaring his love for her. Palmer and Queen often went on buggy rides during their courtship. They discovered that they had much in common. For one thing, they shared Quaker beliefs and traditions.

When Palmer was away, he sent Queen letters full of dreams and visions of a future in the West. He told her of the beautiful mountains he had seen, and his plans to build a home in the Rockies—a grand castle with glorious views. If this lovely young lady would become his wife, they could share a beautiful future together.

William once wrote to Queen about a dream he had, not while asleep, but with eyes wide open. "Shall I tell it to you?" he asked. "I thought how fine it would be to have a little railroad a few hundred miles in length, all under one's own control with one's friends, to have no jealousies and contests and differing policies." In Palmer's vision, he planned to hire loyal friends and people he admired to run his railroad, including "a host of good fellows from my regiment," referring to his Civil War troop.

Queen was accustomed to life in New York society. Would she like life in the Wild West? Would she share his passion for railroading and wide open spaces? What if she rejected his proposal of marriage?

Palmer's other plans moved forward quickly. In July 1869, after he saw Pikes Peak for the first time, he set his sights on the eastern foot of the mountain to build a new colony. He wrote of his approach riding the Kansas Pacific, "Pikes Peak never looked grander or more beautiful. The Garden of the Gods fascinated my companions of the eastern frontier so that they bubbled over with enthusiasm." He hoped Queen would have the same reaction.

In another letter, Palmer wrote, "Riding as usual on top of the coach I got wet, but what of that? One can't behold the Rocky Mountains in a storm every day." He was in love with the "free air and lonely plains" of the West as much as he was with his Queen. He chose a spot in a beautiful secluded valley near Garden of the Gods to build his new home. In his excitement, he told Queen she would choose names for all natural rock formations nearby, and she did.

His campaign to win her heart was relentless. "Could one live in constant view of these grand mountains without being elevated by them into a lofty plane of thought and purpose?" he wrote. How could she resist?

Palmer invited Queen and her father to visit the new settlement. They arrived in April 1870. An early spring storm hid the beautiful mountain views. Harsh cold winds mixed rain with snow. Although Queen did not "bubble over with enthusiasm," Palmer was not discouraged even when she returned to New York.

In June 1870, the U.S. Census listed "William Palmer, age 33, Construction Director for the Kansas

Pacific Railroad" living in Denver. His widowed mother and his sister had moved from Pennsylvania to live with him. His passport applications described him as five-feet ten-inches tall, with hazel eyes, reddish brown hair, oval face, square chin, and a moustache, born in Delaware, living in Colorado, occupation, "railroad man."

In September 1870, Palmer's Kansas Pacific construction crew finished the railroad between Kansas and Denver. The train came chuffing into town at fif-

DENVER CITY.

A sketch of "Denver City" as Palmer would have known it. This sketch appeared in Harper's New Monthly Magazine, June 1867.

teen miles per hour. Now, Denver was connected by rail to the rest of the country. The Denver Pacific expanded north to Cheyenne, Wyoming, connecting with the busy East-West Union Pacific.

With this landmark achieved, Palmer shifted his focus. He was serious about building a railroad line south from Denver through Colorado and New Mexico, to El Paso, Texas, a distance of 875 miles. He did not plan to stop there. His line would extend to Mexico City, the capital of Mexico.

Palmer could not convince Kansas Pacific management to build a railroad into Mexico. To fulfill his vision, he left Kansas Pacific and started his own company. On October 27, 1870, the Denver & Rio Grande Railroad began operations. A new railroad was born.

Palmer began the complicated process of raising money. He purchased land grants and rights-of-way from the United States government to build his railroad across Colorado. But first, he took a break from his ambitious business endeavors to attend to an important personal issue. He wished to settle his position with Queen Mellen.

In spite of Queen's less than favorable first glimpse of Colorado, she accepted William's proposal of marriage. On November 8, 1870, the couple was married in Queen's father's home in Flushing.

For their honeymoon trip, Mr. and Mrs. Palmer traveled to England. In London, William scheduled business meetings over dinners. Their journals indicated that Queen attended most of these business dinners, but missed a few when she felt "slightly unwell." In spite of William's business meetings, the honeymoon couple enjoyed walks, carriage rides, meals, and cultural attractions.

While in London, Palmer met with his friend and business partner, William Bell. The men visited engineers to learn about various gauges, or widths, of railroad lines. One train in Wales was only two feet wide. Palmer and Bell decided to use a three-foot-wide narrow gauge for their new railroad.

Standard gauge rails were four-feet, eight-and-one-half-inches wide. A narrower gauge and light rails would be needed for the tight turns and steep **grades** to build a railroad through canyons and passes of the Rocky Mountains. The narrow gauge lightweight rails were ordered from Wales. Financing was arranged through Dr. Bell's contacts in London, Palmer's associates in Philadelphia, and William Mellen's in New York City.

*Queen Palmer photographed near the time of her marriage to
William Palmer in 1870.*

As soon as he could, William Palmer traveled west to begin work as president of his own railroad, the Denver and Rio Grande. Queen stayed at her father's New York home. In Colorado, Palmer was fully occupied with his new company, building a new settlement at the foot of Pikes Peak, and construction of a new home for himself and Queen.

The first stake to hold the first rail for Palmer's new train line was hammered into the ground on July 28, 1871. The new company became widely known as the D&RG. Much work lay ahead.

5　A City is Born

In addition to building a railroad, Palmer had great plans for a new city. He wrote to his friend, General Simon Cameron, "My theory for this place is that it should be made the most attractive place for homes in the West; a place for schools, colleges, sciences, and first-class newspapers, and everything the above implies."

By August 1871, Palmer's own railroad connected Denver to the newly laid out town known as the Fountain Colony, later named Colorado Springs. Only one house existed when the train first reached the location of the new town.

Within a year, Palmer had pushed the Denver & Rio Grande south to connect with the town of Pueblo. From Pueblo, the railroad turned west toward coal fields near Canon City along the Arkansas River.

Palmer built the railroad to serve the needs of mining settlements. With the coming of the railroad, small mountain communities prospered. His narrow gauge line was known as the "Baby Railroad."

Queen Palmer arrived in Colorado Springs in October 1871, with her father and stepmother and their six children. William Palmer was away on a railroad survey when they arrived after their long journey across the continent. Dr. Bell met the group at the railroad station and took them to his cabin.

Palmer and Queen's new home was not yet near completion. For a few months, the couple slept in tents, then moved into the barn behind the building site. This provided a challenge for Palmer's bride from New York who was used to modern conveniences.

Although building a new town was a big job, it seemed an attainable goal for a man who built railroads. He asked Queen to teach the children of the settlers in the area. She taught the first classes in a rented building and hired other teachers until a school district could be established. Queen embraced her teaching job with enthusiasm. Streets in the new city were named at Queen's suggestion for mountain and rivers, such as Cascade, Nevada, Tejon, Pikes Peak, Colorado, Bijou, and Cucharras.

The new colony, which attracted many immigrants and visitors from England, became known as "Little London". A friend of the Palmers, Rose Kingsley, arrived from England with her brother. While they lived in a cabin with an attached tent, she wrote extensive journals, which were published under the title *South By West* in 1873. She wrote, "These plains run east to Kansas, without a single tree, for 400 miles…The streets and blocks are only marked out by a furrow turned with the plough, and indicated faintly by a wooden house, finished, or in process of building, here and there, scattered over half a mile of prairie. About twelve houses and shanties are inhabited, most of them being unfinished, or run up for temporary occupation; and there are several tents dotted about also."

After a visit to the Palmer's unfinished home, Rose wrote, "the P's [Palmers] are building a most charming large house: but till it is finished they live in a sort of picnic way, in rooms 10 x 10, partitioned off from the loft over the stable! There was just room for us all four to sit at tea, and we had great fun. There were four cups, but no saucers; and we had borrowed two forks from the restaurant, so that we each had one."

Rose Kingsley wrote about Queen's job as Colorado Springs' only teacher. "Mrs. P has undertaken to begin a school for the colonists' children, and opened it this morning. I went up before she arrived and found seven children all in great excitement about their teacher. The school is some way up the town side; a pretty three-roomed house which Mrs. P. has rented till a regular school-house can be built. The school is flourishing, and everyone is pleased."

In February 1872, the Palmers' new house was ready. They named it "Glen Eyrie," meaning *valley of the eagle's nest*. The community was growing as well. A new Colorado Springs Hotel opened and was also ready for operation. Palmer started a newspaper called *Out West*.

A month later, Palmer took Queen and Rose Kingsley on a trip into Mexico. It was more than a sightseeing adventure. Palmer was planning for future railroad construction and meeting with government officials.

After extending his railroad line from Colorado to Laredo, Texas, Palmer hoped to build it all the way to

In 1871, General Palmer built this home for Queen on an estate they named Glen Eyrie located north of the Garden of the Gods near Colorado Springs. The house and grounds were completely renovated in 1881.

Mexico City. This would require laying hundreds of miles of narrow gauge rails across the Mexican Plateau. Another line would connect Mexico to the west coast. By building the railways south into Mexico, Palmer hoped to expand trade and interaction between the United States and Mexico.

The trip began by traveling to California, where the group boarded a steamship to the Mexican coast. On the ship, the Palmers' met Porfirio Diaz. In later years, Diaz became president of Mexico and helped Palmer with railroad development.

The rest of the trip was by stagecoach and horseback across the rugged plains to Mexico City. It was a **turbulent** time for Mexico. The trip involved hardships and the danger of encounters with robbers and **revolutionaries.** Once they reached Mexico City, Palmer met with local businessmen. He created **alliances** between the Mexican and American governments. He rode for miles on horseback to study the terrain to plan railroad routes over unfamiliar territory.

After several months in Mexico, the group returned to the United States. Queen did not feel well. When she learned she was going to have a baby, she decided to stay in New York. Palmer returned to Colorado. In late October 1872, she gave birth to their first child, Elsie.

Queen returned to Glen Eyrie, joining her father's family there. Her stepmother had a baby girl the same year. Not long after the birth of the baby, Queen's

Queen Palmer in Mexican attire perhaps photographed during the Palmers' extended visit to Mexico in 1872.

father died. Now Palmer was head of two households. William Palmer accepted the added responsibility of caring for and raising his father-in-law's second family of children.

The Palmers settled into making Glen Eyrie a happy place. It was a lively home full of activity, children, and pets. Queen was a charming hostess, a good household manager, and supportive of her husband's business activities.

Palmer started his railroad in a prosperous economy. However, by 1873, an **economic slump** caused a financial panic in Colorado. Money was scarce. The Palmers moved from Glen Eyrie into a smaller house in Colorado Springs six miles away. It was easier to manage a home in town than their remote location of Glen Eyrie. In 1879, the first Colorado Springs city directory listed President of the D&RGRW, Gen'l Wm. J. Palmer, and gave his address as Glen Eyrie.

In 1880, following a high-altitude sight-seeing trip to Leadville, Queen Palmer had a heart attack. She was only thirty years old. Later that year, in spite of her frail health, she gave birth to her second child, Dorothy.

In 1876, Queen Palmer was photographed wearing a mountaineering costume.

Queen's days of hiking and adventure in the high country of Colorado were over. Weakened by the heart attack, she traveled to lower elevations for several months at a time, seeking relief for her condition. The following year, she and her daughters went to England where the Palmers' third child, Marjory, was born in November 1881.

6 The Baby Railroad

William Palmer continued to build railroads. Wherever the rails appeared, people followed and towns were built. Native Americans viewed the construction with a combination of curiosity and dread. The steel rails with their trains fascinated them. The new people on their land frightened and angered them. Inevitable conflicts between the native peoples and the settlers were a constant threat to both groups.

Rail construction was halted temporarily during the 1873 economic depression, but by 1876, Palmer's railroad had pushed into Southern Colorado. By 1878, Palmer's Baby Railroad was more than three-hundred miles long and the longest narrow gauge road in the world. His train pushed "through the Rockies, not around them." This became the D&RG motto.

In 1879, the Colorado Coal and Iron Company was formed in Pueblo. Now, the iron rails could be manufactured in Colorado. In 1880, the South Pueblo Iron Works began operating. It would later become Colorado Fuel and Iron Company. Big industry had arrived on the rails in Southern Colorado.

Palmer planned for his narrow gauge to extend all the way to Mexico City. He admired Mexico and its people. However, he was unable to build south across New Mexico to make the connection. The rival Santa Fe had secured that territory for their own railroad lines.

In Colorado, Palmer continued expanding his narrow gauge lines into the mountains. Two railroads, the Atcheson, Topeka, and Santa Fe (known as the Santa Fe), and the Kansas Pacific, competed for railroad routes. Palmer surveyed critical routes to the Leadville mining district. The railroad companies competed to build a western extension of existing railroad through the steep and scenic canyons of Royal Gorge to reach Leadville. Construction was difficult along the narrow canyons that banked the Arkansas River.

A railroad war began. Rivals Santa Fe and the D&RG both wished to build tracks from Canon City through the Royal Gorge canyon. A profitable connection could then be completed to the mining district in Leadville. When the companies clashed over ownership of rights to the narrow river canyon, railroad building came to a halt.

D&RG tracks ended just short of Canon City. Residents became angry and frustrated that railroad access did not reach their town. They worried they would be forced to pay for the completion of the tracks.

Bad feelings spread. Palmer's D&RG punished the Santa Fe by raising the lease rate charged for the Santa Fe to use D&RG tracks. The Santa Fe did not repair tracks they leased from the D&RG. Each company lured workers away from the opposing railroad by offering higher wages.

When the case went to court, a judge ruled on April 4, 1880, that the Santa Fe unfairly blocked construction in the Royal Gorge canyon. Although no blood was shed, harsh words were exchanged, and tools were thrown into the river by rival construction crews. Telegraph lines were cut and mail service was disrupted.

The hostility between the railroad companies was known as the "Bloodless Railroad War" or the "Royal

Gorge War." After all the disruption, Palmer built his railroad through the beautiful Royal Gorge canyon. The D&RG constructed a hanging bridge, an engineering marvel which provided stability for the tracks, where the riverbank was too narrow for rails.

Fierce competition continued among the railroad companies. Palmer pushed his work crews to their limits. He sometimes held up their wages to use the money for further development. Sometimes maintenance of the rails was overlooked. The railroad pushed forward and grew too fast to sustain the Baby Railroad's reputation as safe and reliable.

Palmer's D&RG survived. Many railroad companies did not. In addition to competition from other railroad companies, Palmer struggled to balance promises to shareholders and government bondholders with the realities and difficulties of railroad development. He remained optimistic and aggressive and kept his railroad in the race for expansion routes.

Palmer extended his routes in many directions. He hired 2,000 men to work on a new line from Alamosa to Durango in 1880. The townspeople of Durango hoped this would not be a case of "throttling." *Throttling* was the term used when a train line ended before it reached

IN THE ROYAL GORGE, GRAND CANON OF THE ARKANSAS, COLORADO
SPANNED BY THE HIGHEST BRIDGE IN THE WORLD

*The Denver & Rio Grande Western in the Royal Gorge Canyon as
depicted on a 1920s postcard.*

a town forcing the town to pay for the last miles of track into town. The line to Durango was completed without throttling the town. D&RG's greatest year for growth came in 1881. Southwest Colorado was connected to Denver by 495 miles of rails.

In 1881, the *Rocky Mountain News* said of the D&RG, "Its progress and success has exceeded the wildest hope of its friends. It is pushing its way toward Old Mexico with amazing rapidity, and with its various branches and extensions, is covering all of the Centennial state with a perfect network of steel track."

To continue the expansion, Palmer needed money. He wanted to build another new line to Grand Junction and into Utah. Jay Gould, a powerful railroad tycoon who owned the Union Pacific Railroad, also wanted to expand into Utah. Gould needed a connecting line from east to west and wished to absorb the D&RG. If he spread false rumors that D&RG finances were unstable, the price of D&RG stock would fall. Gould could then take over. His company did not succeed in taking over the D&RG until two decades later.

In the meantime, Palmer started a new branch line. It was called the Denver and Rio Grande Western

Railway Company, known as the Western, or D&RGW. This line would connect Salt Lake City, Utah, with the D&RG at the Colorado state line when it came north from Durango through Grand Junction.

The pattern was familiar by now. Railroad companies raced each other to connect east and west. Money and manpower were stretched thin. Investment interest payments and worker paychecks were late. Salt Lake City waited anxiously for its connection by rail to the rest of the United States.

On March 30, 1883, with much celebration, the lines from east and west met at Green River, Utah. Now the trip from Salt Lake City to Denver was a thirty-five hour ride through 735 miles of winding mountains with fabulous scenery. The D&RG now claimed thirteen hundred miles of railroad routes.

Palmer's associate Dr. William Bell's description of railroad construction was reprinted in 1975 in National Geographic's *We Americans:*

> Reporter William A. Bell watched in awe as Irishmen, Indians, Chinese, Mexicans, and drifters of every stripe stretched tendrils of the Eastern railroad web into the West. Crews with shovels and buckets

readied the roadbed. Teamsters reined up wagonloads of ties, then giddapped back for more as gangs thumped ties and plates into position.

Sweating men laid the rails with drill-team precision. At a command, two grabbed a rail from a waiting wagon and hefted it forward. Two more took hold, then two more, until 12 were trotting to the ties with some 30 feet of iron. 'Halt!' barked a boss, like as not an ex-Union army officer; 'Down!' and the rail found its home. Spike drivers locked it to the ties, three blows to a spike, ten spikes to a rail. 'On with another!' and four rails a minute clanged down in a brawny ballet.

Rails for tomorrow roll in on those laid today, and behind them, the ungainly boxcars with bunks where tired **gandy dancers**—railroad laborers nicknamed for tools they used—could dream of a golden spike. [A ceremonial golden spike was driven into the roadbed when lines from east and west connected.]

Many years later, in a speech to D&RG employees, Dr. Bell said, "The present generation has little conception of the work done by General Palmer. It is apt to think of later men as the builders of the Rio

Courtesy Special Collections, Tutt Library, Colorado College, Colorado Springs, Colorado

Until a fall from horseback in 1906 left him paralyzed, General Palmer rode daily. He was often accompanied on rides by his much loved Great Danes.

Grande. The road is his monument. Those who followed have built on the foundation he laid."

A sketch entitled "Laying the Rails" illustrated an article in Harper's New
Monthly Magazine, June 1867.

7 On the Right Track

With an important connection across the nation at last accomplished, the Denver & Rio Grande railroad reviewed its problems. They were many. A new board of directors criticized Palmer for expanding routes and extensions too quickly. He was asked to resign as president, which he did on August 9, 1883.

At the time, the Colorado Springs *Daily Gazette* said, "The resignation of General W.J. Palmer of the presidency of the Denver & Rio Grande railway was tendered to the board of directors at their meeting today and accepted. Resolutions of regret at his retirement were unanimously carried." Frederick Lovejoy, an Easterner from Philadelphia was appointed the new president of the D&RG. Lovejoy resented Palmer and relished moving ahead without him.

Palmer's resignation was not a retirement. He had other goals. He maintained his position as director of the D&RG and was re-elected as president of the branch company, the Rio Grande Western. All of Palmer's energy went into the Western as an extension of the D&RG. He pushed the Western further across the Utah plains, connecting Salt Lake City to Ogden in 1883.

To expand the Western line, Palmer knew he still needed to work with the D&RG. By connecting their routes, the two companies could expand together. He also wanted to protect the railroad property in Colorado he had worked so hard to obtain and develop.

When it became more difficult for Palmer to work with the new management at the D&RG, he resigned his position on the board of directors. Lovejoy, the new board president, tore up a critical mile of railroad tracks that had been laid from Grand Junction west to the Utah border. This paralyzed Palmer's western route to Salt Lake City.

Both railroad lines suffered financially. They went into **receivership** until new financing could be arranged. Construction was at a standstill. There was no money to pay employees or to repair the damage caused by Lovejoy's destructive tantrum. Colorado industry depended on the Baby Railroad and hoped it would be up and running again soon.

Palmer's interest in Mexico was revived. Under Palmer's friend, Mexican President Diaz, Mexico became a safer place to travel and more attractive to investors. Although Palmer never built into Mexico, he helped plan and establish the Mexican Central Railway that constructed a connecting route across Mexico. The Railway became the National Railroad of Mexico.

Palmer was busy at home as well. On June 1, 1883, the Antlers Hotel opened. It was advertised as "Colorado's Pride. A summer and winter Resort." The luxury hotel was Palmer's pet project. It featured bathrooms and closets on each floor, and elevators to the top floors.

Palmer's business partner, Dr. Bell, managed the seventy-five room hotel. The hotel's name was inspired by Bell's collection of trophy animals, many with impressive antlers, on display in the lobby. With train routes complete and a new five-story **Queen Anne-style** hotel, Colorado Springs became a popular resort destination for tourists and visitors.

15687. Pikes Peak Avenue, Colorado Springs, Colorado
Pikes Peak in the Distance

The original Antlers Hotel, Pikes Peak Avenue, Colorado Springs, burned in 1898. The rebuilt resort hotel is shown as it looked in the 1910s.

In 1886, the D&RG was sold. The Western emerged from receivership and William Palmer resumed control. Passengers waited patiently for their opportunity to ride the meandering Baby Train from Salt Lake City east, "through the Rockies, not around them," and on to Denver.

A competing line, the Midland Railway, pushed toward Aspen and Leadville. The D&RG raced to complete an extension from Glenwood Springs to Aspen. When the route was finished, residents of the Aspen mining camp celebrated in their favorite way. They lit bonfires and set off dynamite blasts.

A new president took charge of the D&RG. Lovejoy was gone. David H. Moffat took over with an aggressive new management policy. He planned to dig a 9,000-foot-long tunnel for trains through the rock-solid Continental Divide. The Moffat Tunnel opened in 1928 and was named for David Moffat.

Transcontinental trains arrived at the Colorado border on standard gauge rails. To cross Colorado, either the freight load was transferred to a narrow gauge train, or if a third rail had been added to the narrow gauge roadbed, the train continued on. Narrow gauge rails weighed between thirty-five and forty pounds. Regular gauge rails weighed sixty-five to seventy pounds, and were slightly taller. The uneven third rail caused trains to tilt. This created uneven wear and the possibility of **hot box** accidents when fuel in the locomotive slid to one side as the train shifted.

Moffat's solution was to make the new direct line across the Rocky Mountains all standard gauge. In 1887, Moffat ordered 21,000 tons of steel rails, and twenty-seven locomotives with freight and passenger cars. Investors poured in $6 million to cover the expense. The changeover of Colorado railroads to standard gauge took several years. Today three

Courtesy Joyce B. Lohse

A D&RG locomotive at the Colorado Railroad Museum in Golden, Colorado. The locomotive sits on a track that is both standard and narrow gauge.

narrow gauge railroad short lines are still in use in Colorado: the Durango and Silverton Railroad, the Cumbres and Toltec Railroad, and the Georgetown Loop Railroad.

Know More!

Train Gauges and Types

William Palmer's narrow gauge "Baby Railroad" was a novelty in the American West and the pride of the Denver & Rio Grande. From his research in Great Britain, Palmer gained important knowledge about building a train line on narrow three-foot-wide rails, rather than the four-foot-eight-and-a-half-inch wide standard gauge. Narrow gauge rails were lighter weight for construction. Their train cars and locomotives were smaller and lighter to navigate the twists and turns of the rugged Rocky Mountains. Passengers liked them because sleeping cars were narrower, single berths they did not need to share.

Each steam engine was assigned an identification number, displayed prominently with the company name on the front and side. Type of wheel arrangement was described by a number, such as 2-8-2, using the Whyte notation system. The number described the leading pilot wheels in front, power or drive wheels in the middle, and support, or trailing, wheels under the firebox and cab. Higher numbers meant it was a larger locomotive.

Was the narrow gauge the best idea for Colorado railroads? What problems were encountered? Increase your railroad awareness by observing trains you see as you travel.

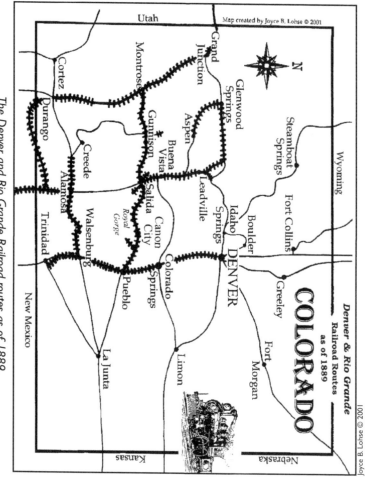

The Denver and Rio Grande Railroad routes as of 1889.

8 The Nomad

While he was courting Queen, William Palmer discussed his plans in his letters to her. In a letter dated January 17, 1870, Palmer told Queen about another plan. "Then I would have a nice house-car made, just convenient for you and me…to travel up and down when business demanded, and this car would contain every convenience of living while in motion."

Most of Palmer's dreams and plans were realized. Some were not. He had succeeded in connecting Colorado's railroad system to the rest of the nation. Development was booming in the new Centennial State, and his beautiful new city of Colorado Springs was thriving under his planning and management.

Fulfilling his promise to Queen, Palmer built a beautiful home at Glen Eyrie. In 1881, Glen Eyrie underwent major renovations based on Queen's designs and suggestions. Palmer added several improvements to the grounds. A rustic schoolhouse was constructed. Railroad rivalries were so strong, Palmer worried that competing railroad companies might kidnap his children. His daughters studied in the safety of the little schoolhouse.

Palmer built an electric power plant for the house. An ice house and a **creamery** were set up, where ice cream was made to the delight of the children. When Palmer heard about **pasteurization** of milk, he traveled to France to learn how to use the process in his dairy.

Palmer was interested in landscaping and loved trees and flowers. During construction of his railroads, he planted seeds to grow thousands of trees along the routes. Plants destroyed in construction were replaced and existing growth was preserved when possible. Palmer served as president of the International Society of **Arboriculture.** John Blair, a famous Scottish landscape architect, designed arched stone bridges and ponds at Glen Eyrie, as well as in parks and at other locations in the new city. Flower gardens, trees, a greenhouse, and a roof garden were added to the grounds.

After the Glen Eyrie renovations were completed, Queen followed her doctor's advice and moved to a lower altitude. She spent two hard winters in New York City, then moved to England with her daughters in 1886. Her last visit to Glen Eyrie was in 1885.

Queen and her girls enjoyed living in England. They entertained many visitors and friends, including a popular American painter living in Europe, John Singer Sargent. He painted a strikingly beautiful portrait in 1889 of Queen's teenage daughter, "Miss Elsie Palmer." It is on display at the Colorado Springs Fine Arts Center.

Palmer stayed in close touch with his family by visiting them in England at least once a year and by frequent letter writing. Sometimes while he was in England, the family traveled to Europe. They visited France, Italy, Switzerland, and Germany. Still, he must have been sad living alone in Colorado.

The railroad kept Palmer busy. As he had dreamed of doing, he used a narrow gauge railroad car named the *Nomad* for his travels. Built in 1878, the car was fifty-feet-long and eight-feet-wide and was part of a three-car train. The first car contained a kitchen and **berths** for the crew. The middle car had two upper and two lower berths. The last car was Palmer's private living quarters.

Palmer became a nomad of the rails. When he traveled, the *Nomad* provided the comforts of home. Sometimes an additional engine was needed to haul the heavy three-car train. The steam-heated private car was luxurious. It was decorated with cut glass, silver serving pieces, deep red upholstery and mahogany furnishings. The car had a council room, a full bed, and a lavatory or bathroom of sorts. A glassed-in observation area at the end of the car contained gauges and a speed meter. By looking into side mirrors, he could see the train cars behind him on curves.

By 1890, the D&RG was changing over to standard gauge rails. The *Nomad* was built to ride the narrow gauge. After a decade of use, the *Nomad* was placed on display at the Denver & Rio Grande railroad yard in Durango, Colorado. Palmer obtained use of a conventional-sized train car named the *Ballyclare*. It allowed for farther-reaching journeys due to its standard gauge.

In 1894, Palmer's oldest daughter, Elsie, visited her father in Colorado. She joined him on his travels around the countryside aboard his private train. She must have enjoyed the fun and adventure of riding the rails in the luxurious little house on train wheels before she returned home to her sisters and her mother in England.

9 Glen Eyrie

Near the end of 1894, William Palmer received tragic news. Queen was gravely ill in Sussex, England. Palmer took a train to New York, then booked passage on a steamship across the Atlantic Ocean. Queen died two days after Christmas and before Palmer arrived. She was forty-four years old. Queen was buried in England, but her remains were later moved to Colorado Springs.

Queen Palmer lived in Colorado Springs for less than half of her married life. While she lived in Colorado, Queen showed an adventurous spirit and a cultured style. She valued education and shared her knowledge and musical talent when she started the first school.

A pioneer in her own right, Queen was involved in planning their new home and community. She named local landmarks and city streets. Queen ventured to new territory and made a home far from all that was familiar to her for as long as her health allowed. Colorado Springs school district named Queen Palmer Elementary School at 1921 E. Yampa Street, in her honor for her work as the city's first school teacher.

Queen's passing from the living world brought her family closer together. William Palmer's three daughters came home to Colorado to live in Glen Eyrie. With his girls in residence and entering adulthood, new life came to the mansion. They helped manage the estate and assisted with entertaining and hospitality. Elsie was twenty-two; Marjory and Dorothy were in their mid-teens. When they all arrived in 1895, Glen Eyrie was far removed from the wooden house under construction where Queen camped with her new husband a quarter of a century earlier. The house was an impressive three-story home with twenty-two rooms.

Palmer shared his good fortune and the beautiful setting of his home by hosting festive parties. The rambling mansion contained rooms both large and cozy, many with their own fireplaces. It was one of the first buildings in the country to install electric lighting. A great hall with high-beamed ceilings, which he called his "Book Hall," was the gathering place for balls and music. Everything he needed could be found on the grounds of his mountain home.

William J. Palmer's daughters—Marjory, Elsie, and Dorothy.

Glen Eyrie was home to several children. Palmer raised his own daughters and was also responsible for the children of his father-in-law. When William Mellen died, he left his second wife with the children to raise. Palmer made them a part of his family. Glen Eyrie was a place to share joys and sorrows with his daughters, a place to entertain visitors, a place to rejuvenate and renew, to meditate in private and celebrate in public. Glen Eyrie was Palmer's retreat and sanctuary.

A reserved man, Palmer had a strong will and was steadfast when dealing with disappointment and failure. While he was away traveling in Europe in 1898, he received word that the Antlers Hotel had burned down. The fire was started by cinders that blew from the railroad depot and landed on the roof of the hotel. He returned home to a hotel in ruins.

Palmer rebuilt the Antlers Hotel. The new hotel was bigger, better, and grander than the first one. Visitors were eager to enjoy the luxurious hospitality and climb the marble stairway in the new Antlers Hotel. When it opened in 1901, the 230-room resort became a social center for Colorado Springs. It was a big success.

Palmer's railroad career came to an end that year.

He sold his interest in the D&RG for $6 million—a huge profit. Palmer thought of a unique way to celebrate his successful career in railroading. He decided to give away $1 million to the men who built the railroad.

With a stack of railroad passes, Palmer rode the train to visit old friends. He found people he hired in the early days of his narrow gauge construction. Then, he surprised them by giving them a portion of the profits from the sale of the railroad. Imagine the surprise of hardscrabble railroad employees when the famous railroad pioneer stepped down from his private rail car. Palmer handed his gift to the surprised workers before quickly retreating back inside his private train car.

A 1901 tourist brochure for the Denver and Rio Grande Railroad raved about Colorado. "The Scenic Line of the World," said the following: "Scenery, altitude, sunshine and air constitute the factors which are rapidly making Colorado the health and pleasure grounds of the world. Here the glowing sun shines three hundred fifty-seven days of the average year, and it blends with the crisp, electric mountain air to produce a climate matchless in the known world. Next to climate, Colorado excels the world in scenery. No pen can portray, no brush can picture, the majestic grandeur of the Rockies."

Palmer believed, "A man must go to the mountains for health, but also to get a true insight into things." Pioneers, pilgrims, and patients all found their way to the town he founded, often arriving on the railroads he built.

10 Colorado Springs Comes of Age

After the turn of the twentieth century, the American landscape was changing. More and more automobiles appeared on city streets as they became affordable for citizens. As much as Palmer loved horses and horseback riding, he understood and appreciated the growing importance of the automobile for transportation.

Palmer maintained a busy and vigorous lifestyle. His home outside of Colorado Springs was a welcoming retreat. His three daughters spent time with him when they could and helped entertain guests. When he took time out from his frequent travels, Palmer enjoyed spending time outdoors on his spacious grounds, tending plants, playing with his dogs, and riding his horses.

Hamlin Garland, a guest at Glen Eyrie, wrote this account of a party around 1900:

> Invited to a garden party at the Glen, we entered through a most beautiful garden in which all the native shrubs and wildflowers had been assembled and planted with exquisite art...people were streaming in over the mountain road...The General, tall, soldierly, clothed in immaculate linen and wearing a broad white Western hat, was receiving his friends...the garden was a wonderland of Colorado plants and flowers, skillfully

Courtesy Colorado Springs Pioneers Museum, Colorado Springs, Colorado

William Palmer with his pet Great Danes at Glen Eyrie.

disposed and scattered along the bases of the cliffs…the towers of the Castle were English, but the plants and blooms surrounding it were native to the Rampart hills.

Know More!

Palmer Pets

Pets were an important part of the Palmer household. Palmer's love of animals began when he lived on a farm in Delaware. He enjoyed riding horseback during his many years of surveying and traveling across prairies and through the mountains. Names of horses mentioned at Glen Eyrie included Don and Schoolboy. He preferred riding horseback to his office in Colorado Springs to riding in a wagon.

Palmer also loved dogs. He owned several Great Danes. Names of his dogs included Dandy, Girton, Infanta, Coelebs, Leo, Ralph, Gellert, Barbara, Mab, Gilbert, Barosra, and Yorick. What do you think inspired these names? Which ones do you like best?

Yorick was especially loved by the children in the household during Palmer's final years. Palmer liked to stage pretend circuses with Yorick as one of the circus animals. Yorick, whose name came from Shakespeare's *Hamlet*, showed Palmer's love for English literature. Yorick, met a sad fate. He was found dead on a path, apparently bitten by a rattlesnake.

Palmer still loved train travel. He continued to be a railroad nomad riding the rails in his private car. The routes he built were now well traveled. The beautiful city of Colorado Springs was prospering.

Palmer donated parcels of land totaling 2,900 acres to the city for an interconnected park system. A partial list of park lands includes Acacia, Antlers, Alamo, Monument Valley, Palmer, Thorndale, High Drive, Bear Creek, North Cheyenne Canyon, Prospect Lake parks. In addition, he donated the land for Colorado College, the Colorado School for the Deaf and Blind, Colorado School of Forestry in Manitou Park, roads and trails, libraries, churches, and hospitals. He made large donations during his lifetime and with the gift, offered his plans for future use and development. He arranged that the city have open space to maintain its attractive appearance and outstanding views.

In 1901, a Century Chest, or time capsule, was created and entrusted to Colorado College with instructions that it not be touched for one hundred years. After New Year's Day 2001, the time capsule was opened. Among newspapers, photos, and documents, it contained a letter from William J. Palmer written in 1901 from Glen Eyrie.

Colorado Springs was twenty-five-years old and Palmer was sixty-five when the letter was written. The letter describes land he donated to Colorado Springs for open space. He mentions land which would become Monument Valley Park and Palmer Park, and also Garden of the Gods. About the growth of the area, he said, "In the half decade which has elapsed since, the place has grown more in population and wealth, I think, than in any previous five years. And no cloud can now be seen hanging over to check its

The entrance to Palmer Hall, Colorado College, Colorado Springs, Colorado.

Courtesy Joyce B. Lohse

The Palmer Mansion at Glen Eyrie, now owned by The Navigators and used as a Christian conference center.

increasing prosperity. The population of the town is now say 25,000—or perhaps over 30,000 including Colorado City, Manitou and all of the community at this foot of Pike's Peak."

Palmer also commented on the town's parks. He said, "When undisturbed, shrubbery and wild flowers grow naturally in these creek bottoms without irrigation—making it easier to carry out the purpose of affording an open and verdurous space removed from the dust and noise of the streets and roads, yet readily accessible from all parts of the town—where the citizen can come to walk (not ride or drive as that means dust) and his children to play—and all be refreshed by a little taste of country, without going too far afield."

Another of Palmer's projects was thriving when he wrote the letter in 1901. Colorado College had grown from its humble beginnings when it opened with a handful of students May 6, 1874, to more than 250 students by the late 1890s. Palmer Hall, a sturdy sandstone classroom building, was dedicated in 1904. Palmer also donated $100,000 to start the Colorado School of Forestry in Manitou Park, once considered the best field laboratory in the country.

At his home, a complete restoration of Glen Eyrie began in 1904. Queen Palmer's original floor plan for the structure was retained. Rock and stone were used to rebuild the entire structure. In keeping with his love of trees and flowers, more plants were installed into the landscape. One-hundred-forty-six trees, 446 shrubs, and 2,000 perennial plants arrived in just one order in 1906.

During the construction, Palmer and his daughters traveled throughout Europe. They visited Italy, France, Spain, and England, collecting **artifacts** and furnishings to decorate the castle. After the facelift, Glen Eyrie was ready for family life, celebrations, and entertaining.

11 A Grand Reunion

Tragedy comes at unexpected times. Palmer survived hardships as a soldier and prisoner of war during the Civil War. He built Colorado Springs and a railroad empire that allowed towns to prosper. He descended deep into the earth to inspect coal and mineral mines. He walked and rode horseback across countless miles of unsettled wilderness. It was **ironic** when a devastating accident occurred on a fine October morning in 1906. Palmer's horse stumbled, and he was thrown hard to the ground. Palmer could not move. His neck was broken, and he was paralyzed.

A man with less endurance might not have survived such a bad fall. At age seventy, Palmer had things yet to do. Although he was severely restricted and handicapped by his injuries, he continued to participate in family and community life.

Through physical therapy, Palmer regained some movement. A chair padded with straw and horsehair was made so that he could sit up and travel comfortably. A rubber bed filled with warm water helped him sleep. His doctor, family, and friends helped him in any way they could. After a visit, a friend wrote, "No one ever saw greater courage under pain and adversity than he displayed."

Palmer took advantage of an important new advancement, the automobile. He owned one of the first White Steamer touring cars. It allowed the stricken railroad pioneer to travel around Colorado Springs from his remote location in Glen Eyrie.

The car became Palmer's main transportation. His brave driver followed Palmer's directions to drive along mountain roads and trails meant for horses, not cars. Palmer enjoyed motoring around Colorado Springs. He often invited guests and visiting children to pile into the car. He especially enjoyed mountain views from the city parks he had donated.

In the years since the Civil War, members of the Anderson Troop had kept in touch with one another. Palmer, who rarely missed their gatherings, was distressed. He would be unable to travel to a reunion of the Fifteenth Pennsylvania Cavalry in Philadelphia. He developed a plan. With help from his daughters, he would invite all 280 men to Colorado Springs.

The plan worked. Realizing many of the veterans would be unable to afford the trip, Palmer spent $50,000 to arrange their travel on a special train. More than one hundred men from the troop showed up in Colorado Springs for their reunion and to visit their ailing general.

The special train arrived on August 20, 1907. Lodging was provided at the Antlers Hotel and in vacant rooms at Colorado College. Sightseeing tours were arranged to Garden of the Gods, Manitou Springs, Cave of the Winds, and the top of Pikes Peak. A concert at Colorado College entertained them, and a reception and banquet at Glen Eyrie fed them. Laughter, tears, and memories were shared. Songs were sung. When it was over, the men went home with new memories to cherish.

A year after the reunion party, Palmer's daughters, Elsie and Marjory, were engaged to be married. Elsie's wedding was in January 1908 at Glen Eyrie. She married Leopold Hamilton Myers from Cambridge, England. The bride wore an unusual brown wrap decorated with huge bronze buckles and 1,000 tiny bronze animals. The couple traveled to New York, then sailed to England.

Marjory planned to marry a British Army Captain named Wellesley in June. Palmer arranged to travel to England with his daughter. For the difficult journey, Palmer brought along his personal physician, Dr. Henry C. Watt. The trip was arranged and they were on their way. After riding the rails he helped build to cross the continent, they took a steamship to England.

Before they reached England, Dr. Watt declared his love for Marjory. He asked her to marry him instead of Wellesley. The wedding in England was called off, but the trip continued. When the visit was over, the group transported Palmer back to Colorado.

Dorothy remained single. She moved to London where she worked as a social worker.

The long journey took its toll on the ailing Palmer, and his health became worse. On March 13, 1909, William Palmer died at his home in Glen Eyrie. His cremated remains were buried in Evergreen Cemetery under a simple headstone of Pikes Peak granite that he had chosen.

Headstone at General Palmer's gravesite in Evergreen Cemetery, Colorado Springs, Colorado.

The family held a quiet ceremony, in accordance with his reserved style and wishes. Queen's remains were brought home from England and buried next to her husband's.

12 Palmer Remembered

William Palmer believed in making donations in person. During his lifetime, he donated more than half of his fortune for the betterment of Colorado Springs and the state of Colorado. His presence is still strongly felt in the area.

Palmer's estate was divided among his three daughters and their families. While he was alive, he gave away between four and five million dollars. Donations included parks and open space in Colorado Springs, gifts to Rio Grande Western railroad employees, private charities, Colorado College, the Hampton Institute, and others.

Palmer donated land for the town of Palmer Lake between Colorado Springs and Denver. The community grew around its railroad station. When the Baby Railroad first **traversed** the Monument Divide, the steam engine took on water from the nearby lake to gain power. The picturesque foothill setting became a rest stop and popular destination for picnics, hiking, and boating. Cost for a roundtrip ticket from Denver was one dollar.

After his death, Palmer's Glen Eyrie estate was vacant. Then his daughters sold it. In 1953, a group called The Navigators bought it for $340,000. They maintained and restored the mansion and estate to its former splendor. In 1971, Glen Eyrie became incorporated into Colorado Springs. Under ownership and management of The Navigators, the estate continues as a Christian conference center, retreat, and camp. The mansion is open for guided tours and afternoon tea. Overnight lodging is available, and hikers can explore trails on the 792-acre estate.

The Denver and Rio Grande train station survives as a restaurant. Diners watch the railroad tracks through large windows. Nearby, D&RG engine number #168 sits by a walking path in a park where it can be seen at close range.

Colorado College continues as a center for higher education. Palmer Hall is located in the center of the campus. Palmer is honored in the building with a painted portrait and a bronze bas-relief. The bronze tablet shows Palmer with one of his Great Danes. Students rub the dog's nose on exam days for good luck. The nose is now shiny against the dull metal background. Duplicates of the metal tablet created in 1929, were installed in railroad stations in Mexico City, Salt Lake City, and Denver. The tablets contain this inscription:

William Jackson Palmer – 1836-1909

Union Cavalry General, pioneer railroad builder, prophet of Colorado's greatness. He mapped the route of three transcontinental railways, supervised the building of the first road to Denver, organized and constructed the State's industries, cherished its beauties, founded Colorado Springs, fostered Colorado College, and served our Sister Republic of Mexico with sympathy and wisdom in developing its national railways.

Palmer's interest in higher education reached far. He supported the Hampton Institute in Virginia. When the college was established in 1861, classes were taught under an oak tree in defiance of a law prohibiting education for African Americans. It provided rare opportunities for learning. The school still exists as Hampton University. In 1929, a bronze plaque honoring Palmer was placed in the administration building he helped fund.

Colorado Springs contains many tributes to Palmer. A portrait of Palmer by Hubert Herkomer greets visitors to the Colorado Springs Pioneers Museum. A case contains artifacts from his life. Other Palmer portraits by Herkomer are on display in Colorado College, Penrose Library, and in city offices. John Singer Sargent's painting, "Portrait of Miss Elsie Palmer," or "Young Lady in White," 1889-90, can be seen at the Colorado Springs Fine Arts Center. A portrait of Dorothy Palmer hangs in the Colorado Springs Pioneers Museum.

The McAllister House, built in 1873 by Palmer's friend Henry McAllister, was no doubt visited by Palmer. McAllister was his lifelong friend and business colleague. McAllister's daughter remembered watching through the window as Palmer briskly rode his horse into town, a determined expression on his mustached face, his cape flowing behind him. The

McAllister House is now a museum.

In 1929, a statue of Palmer on his horse was installed at the busy intersection of Platte and Nevada Avenues, very near Palmer High School. The statue of the man on the horse is a wonderful likeness of Palmer. He sits tall and straight in the saddle, his stirrups adjusted in long cavalry style, gazing wistfully toward the mountains. Perhaps the man on the horse is listening for the wail of a distant train whistle, echoing through the foothills, transporting people and goods over the miles of rails he built.

Courtesy Joyce B. Lohse

Timeline

1829 – The first successful commercial locomotive is introduced in America.

1836 – William Jackson Palmer is born at Kinsale Farm, two miles from Leipsic, Kent County, Delaware.

1841 – The Palmer family moves to Philadelphia, PA where William attends school.

1850 – Mary Lincoln "Queen" Mellen is born in Prestonburg, Kentucky.

1853 – William Palmer (16) obtains a job with the Hempfield Railroad in Pennsylvania.

1855 – Palmer (18) travels to England and Europe to conduct railroad research.

1858 – Palmer becomes secretary to the president of the Pennsylvania Railroad.

1861 – William Palmer enters the Civil War, serving as captain in the Union Army.

1862 – Captain Palmer organizes the Fifteenth Pennsylvania Volunteer Cavalry. He is captured and held prisoner in Castle Thunder, Richmond, Virginia.

1863 – Palmer is released from prison and promoted to the rank of colonel in the Union Army.

1865 – Civil War ends. Palmer goes to work for the Kansas Pacific Railroad.

1869 – Railroads from east and west meet at Promontory Point, Utah. Palmer sees Pikes Peak for the first time.

1870 – Kansas Pacific Railroad reaches Denver with Palmer as Construction Director. He marries Mary Lincoln "Queen" Mellen. Denver and Rio Grande narrow gauge railroad begins operations.

1871 – The Denver & Rio Grande Railroad connects Denver and Colorado Springs. The town of Colorado Springs is founded. Queen Palmer opens a school.

1872 – Palmer's railroad reaches Pueblo. Glen Eyrie is built. Daughter Elsie is born in New York.

1874 – Colorado College founded in Colorado Springs.

1878 – Railroad wars fight for rights to the Royal Gorge right-of-way.

1879 – Palmer is director of Colorado Coal and Iron Company, later CF&I, in Pueblo.

1880 – Queen suffers a heart attack after a trip to Leadville. Daughter Dorothy Palmer is born in Colorado Springs.

1881 – Glen Eyrie is renovated.
Queen goes to England where daughter Marjory is born.

1883 – Palmer opens the Antlers Hotel in Colorado Springs. He resigns as president of the D&RG and extends the Western line. East and west railroad routes meet in Utah.

1885 – Palmer helps plan the Mexican National Railway system.

1886 – Queen Palmer and daughters move to England. The D&RG is sold.

1889 – D&RG achieves its maximum narrow gauge routes with 1,861 miles.

1891 – Gold is discovered in Cripple Creek, Colorado.

1894 – Queen Palmer (44) dies in England.

1895 – Palmer's three daughters return with Palmer to live at Glen Eyrie.

1898 – The Antlers Hotel burns.

1901 – Palmer sells his Western line. He donates land to Colorado Springs, including Palmer Park. The rebuilt Antlers Hotel opens.

1904 – Glen Eyrie is rebuilt as a brick and stone castle. Palmer and his daughters travel to Europe. Palmer Hall is built on the Colorado College campus.

1906 – Palmer is paralyzed after a fall from his horse.

1907 – The Fifteenth Pennsylvania Cavalry are guests at Glen Eyrie for a reunion.

1908 – Daughter Elsie marries Leo Hamilton Myers at Glen Eyrie. Palmer travels to England for Marjory's wedding.

1909 – William J. Palmer (72) dies at Glen Eyrie. He is buried in Evergreen Cemetery in Colorado Springs. Queen Palmer's ashes are moved from England and buried in the plot.

Colorado Springs Gazette, August 10, 1883; January 3, 1895; October 28, 1906; July 31, 1921; March 16, 1924; September 1, 1929; April 23, 1937; April 2, 1944.

Colorado Springs, Manitou and Colorado City directory, W. H. H. Raper and Company, August, 1879.

Colorado Springs Pioneers Museum, Colorado Springs, Colorado, William J. Palmer manuscript collection.

Denver & Rio Grande Railroad, "Panoramic Views Along The Line of The D&RG" (brochure), Poole Bros., Chicago, Illinois, 1901, Penrose Library Archives.

Fisher, John S., *A Builder of the West: The Life of General William Jackson Palmer,* Caxton Printers, Caldwell, Idaho, 1939, pp. 162, 178.

Hagerman, Percy, "People I Have Known" (from speech to the El Paso Club), *Gazette Telegraph,* April 2, 1944, p. 1.

Harper's New Monthly Magazine, "Over the Plains to Colorado", June 1867, pp. 1-21.

Harper's New Monthly Magazine, "The General's Story", June 1867, pp. 60-74.

Kingsley, Rose Georgina, *South by West: or, Winter in the Rocky Mountains and Spring in Mexico,* W. Isbister & Co., London, England, 1874.

LeMassena, Robert A., *Rio Grande…to the Pacific!,* Sundance Limited, Denver, Colorado, 1974.

McAllister, Henry, "General William Palmer – Pioneer Engineer", *The Engineers' Bulletin,* Official Bulletin of the Colorado Society of Engineers, Sept-Oct 1929. Speech also included in *William Jackson Palmer – Pathfinder and Builder,* printed by George Foster Peabody, Saratoga Springs, New York, 1931.

McCarthy, Judge Wilson, *General Wm. Jackson Palmer (1836-1909), And the D.&R.G.W. Railroad,* [speech to] The Newcomen Society in North American, New York, New York, 1954.

McGilchrist, Donald, "History of the Gardens Glen Eyrie," 1995, notes and chronologies, Colorado Springs, Colorado.

Miller, Francis Trevelyan, editor-in-chief, *The Photographic History of the Civil War, Volume 7,* The Review of Reviews Co., New York City, 1911.

Navigators brochure, Glen Eyrie, Colorado Springs, Colorado.

New York Times, October 28, 1906: August 18, 1907: January 21, 1908: March 14, 1909.

Newhouse, Elizabeth L., ed., *The Story of America,* National Geographic Society, Washington, D.C., 1984, pp. 147-153.

Noel, Thomas J. and Norman, Cathleen M., *A Pikes Peak Partnership: The Penroses and The Tutts,* University Press of Colorado, Niwot, Colorado, 2000.

Palmer Lake Historical Society, "A Brief History of the Palmer-Divide Area" (flyer), Palmer Lake, Colorado, 2005.

Palmer Memorial Day program, July 31, 1932, Penrose Library Archives.

Panoramic Views Along the Line of the Denver & Rio Grande Railroad, Penrose Public Library Manuscript Collection, 1901.

Peabody, George Foster, *William Jackson Palmer, Pathfinder and Builder,* a compilation of addresses at presentations of bronze bas reliefs and equestrian statue, published privately by Peabody, Saratoga, New York, 1931.

Pikes Peak Library District, *Legends, Labors & Loves of William Jackson Palmer, 1836-1909,* a compilation, Colorado Springs, Colorado, 2009.

Rocky Mountain News, May 14, 1867; October 20, 1870; August 6, 1872; January 1, 1881.

Sawatski, Jim, *The Life and Times of General William Jackson Palmer,* VHS, Colorado Springs Pioneers Museum Foundation, Colorado Springs, Colorado, 2004.

Smith, Linda D., "Glen Eyrie, Palmer's Castle Tribute to Elegance," *Gazette Telegraph,* Colorado Springs, Colorado, August 28, 1982.

Sprague, Marshall, *Newport In The Rockies,* Swallow Press/Ohio University Press, Athens, Ohio, 1961.

Stark, Dolores, "Hectic Adventures Marked Civil War Career of Gen. William Palmer," *The Gasser,* Colorado Interstate Gas Company, Colorado Springs, Colorado, May 1961, pp. 16-19.

Summit County Journal, Breckenridge, Colorado, March 27, 1909.

U.S. Census, Philadelphia County, Pennsylvania, 1860.

U.S. Census, Denver, Colorado, 1870.

U.S. Census, El Paso County, Colorado, 1880 and 1900.

U.S. National Archives and Records, Compiled Military Service File, Civil War documents for William J. Palmer.

Wallace, Liz, *KIVA,* Cheyenne Mountain publication, Colorado Springs, Colorado, Winter, 2003, pp. 4-11.

Wilcox, Rhoda Davis, *The Man On The Iron Horse,* Martin Associates, Manitou Springs, Colorado, 1959.

World Book Multimedia Encyclopedia, World Book Inc., 1998. Articles about Locomotives and Quakers.

Index

Acknowledgments

With gratitude, I thank Leah Davis Witherow and Kelly Murphy at the Colorado Springs Pioneers Museum, Chris Nichol and staff at Penrose Library, railroad expert and historian Art Crawford, Jessy Randolph and Amy Brooks at the Colorado College Tutt Library Archives, Donald McGilchrist of the Navigators, Glen Eyrie historian Len Froisland, and inspiration from my friend, Paul Idleman. I am forever grateful to my publishers, Doris and Tom Baker at Filter Press, my family, my friends, and most of all, Don, for unwavering support.

About the Author

Award-winning author **Joyce B. Lohse** grew up in Illinois. She has lived in the West since 1974. Joyce is the author of a dual biography entitled *First Governor, First Lady: John and Eliza Routt of Colorado*, and biographies of Justina Ford, Emily Griffith, and Margaret (Molly) Brown published in the Now You Know Bios™ series from Filter Press. Joyce, a frequent speaker to history and genealogy groups, also writes history articles for magazines. Learn more about Joyce and her writing projects at *www.lohseworks.com*.

MORE Now You Know Bios

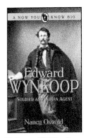

Edward Wynkoop
1831 – 1891
Soldier and Indian Agent
978-0-86541-184-5

Florence Sabin
1871 – 1953
Teacher, Scientist,
Humanitarian
978-0-86541-139-5

Dottie Lamm
1937 –
Former first lady of Colorado
and social activist.
ISBN 978-0-086541-085-5

Emily Griffith
1868 – 1947
Educator and founder of Denver's
Emily Griffith Opportunity School.
ISBN 978-0-86541-077-0

John Denver
1943 – 1997
Singer, songwriter, world-known
performer, and humanitarian.
ISBN 978-0-086541-088-6

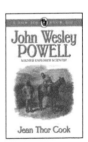

John Wesley Powell
1834 – 1902
Soldier, Explorer, Scientist. Led
the first exploration of the
Grand Canyon.
ISBN 978-0-86541-080-0

Justina Ford
1871 – 1952
The first African-American woman
to practice medicine in CO.
ISBN 978-0-86541-074-9

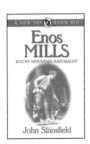

Enos Mills
1870 – 1922
The father of Rocky
Mountain National Park.
ISBN 978-0-86541-072-5

Martha Maxwell
1831 – 1881
Naturalist, innovative
taxidermist, museum builder.
ISBN 978-0-86541-075-6

Molly Brown
1867 – 1932
Heroine of the Titanic and
philanthropist.
ISBN 978-0-86541-081-7

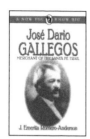

José Dario Gallegos
1830 – 1883
Founder of San Luis,
oldest town in Colorado.
ISBN 978-0-86541-084-8

Chipeta
1843 – 1924
Ute peacemaker and wife
of Chief Ouray.
ISBN 978-0-86541-091-6

Mary Elitch Long
1856 – 1936
Founder of Elitch Gardens
Amusement Park in Denver, CO.
ISBN 978-0-86541-094-7

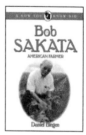

Bob Sakata
1926 –
American farmer and
community leader.
ISBN 978-0-86541-093-0

Susan Anderson
1870 – 1960
Pioneer mountain doctor
By Lydia Griffith
ISBN 978-0-86541-108-1

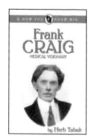

Frank Craig
1877 – 1914
Founded the Brotherly Relief Colony
for destitute consumptives, now the
Craig Rehabilitation Hospital.
ISBN 978-0-86541-092-3

Now You Know Bios are available at your local bookstore,
by calling 888.570.2663, and online at www.FilterPressBooks.com